Midnight Musings

A Collection of Odes & Quotes

Kay S

notionpress.com

INDIA · SINGAPORE · MALAYSIA

Copyright © Kavitha Srinivasan (Kay S) 2023
All Rights Reserved.

ISBN 979-8-88849-069-3

This book has been published with all efforts taken to make the material error-free after the consent of the author. However, the author and the publisher do not assume and hereby disclaim any liability to any party for any loss, damage, or disruption caused by errors or omissions, whether such errors or omissions result from negligence, accident, or any other cause.

While every effort has been made to avoid any mistake or omission, this publication is being sold on the condition and understanding that neither the author nor the publishers or printers would be liable in any manner to any person by reason of any mistake or omission in this publication or for any action taken or omitted to be taken or advice rendered or accepted on the basis of this work. For any defect in printing or binding the publishers will be liable only to replace the defective copy by another copy of this work then available.

Contents

Contents

Contents

© Image by Artie Navarre from Pixabay

Thought for the Day

Today, I express my heartfelt gratitude to the Universe for inspiring me to write its thoughts and I thank you all for inspiring me to be a better version of myself each day. Gratitude and Humanity shall go a long way to define the kind of human being you are. The choice is, of course, Yours. Stay Blessed.

Kay S

Dedication and Gratitude

No creation in this world can be complete without the blessings of the Supreme and the spiritual guides who lead us to him. Hence, it is with utmost humility that I bow down to the Supreme and offer this humble offering of mine where I have attempted to put my thoughts into words in the form of poetry. 'I exist in 'You' wholesomely for you complete my Universe. One of the most important presence in my life is that of my Guru, my spiritual guide, my Baba Jaan. I am greatly indebted and grateful to him and place this at his humble feet as an offering for all the abundance of constant blessings, support, and belief he has in me; I would not be here in this world without his constant presence in my life.

Furthermore, I would not be who and where I am without a few great souls who have been a part of my life and this book would be incomplete but for the acknowledgement of the presence of them in my life. My most humble gratitude and thanks to the master of my soul, my guide, the reason for my meaningful existence today, Khan Saab. I would not be where I am or who I am nor would I have Baba Jaan in my life without you. My heartfelt gratitude to you for staying by me like a rock and always believing in me. I hope you continue to be the lighthouse for me forever. Thank you for the opportunity to exist in your space. You inspire me more than you will ever know.

One of the most important periods of my life has been the chance to become a mother to my wonderful kids. My heartfelt thanks to my lovely children, Sheetal and Shreyas for giving me the chance to have been their mother and always standing by me. I am a better mother because of both of them and you make me proud. Ritika, my darling girl who has my son's heart; thank you for always guiding me through the little creative hurdles that I faced. I love you all loads.

A special thanks and respect to my aunt, Pushpa Iyer who has brought back memories of my mom and taking her place keeps blessing me believing in my capabilities to succeed. My respects to my late parents and all the souls who have always blessed me. Last but not the least, I would like to thank a special person from the bottom of my heart who deserves a special mention and that is my darling little sister, Bhavani Iyer who is my genius critic, my guiding light. You have been a constant support and belief system who always believes that I have the power to conquer the world and I can never be thankful enough to the Universe for making you a part of my life again. My love to all my feline, canine, and avian family that make a part of our extended family.

A very special mention goes to the creator of the cover of this book, Rushabh Nagaraj, a Godson I am extremely proud of. I also owe photo credits to Rushabh along with Rajiv Sukumar, Dr. Vivek Jawali, and Krishnakumar Mahalingam, all people with hearts of gold and photography skills par excellence. Thanks a million, Darling Souls! You inspire me more than you will ever know.

A shout out and heartfelt thanks to each and every one of you, family and friends, who have been a part of my life throughout my journey until today because I would not be who I am without all of you contributing to it. The limitation of space restricts me from mentioning all your names, but you all know who you are. Thank you and God bless you all with abundance of health, happiness, prosperity and success in all that you choose to do in your lives. Always remember, "You are born by chance, your choices define you!"

Kay S

© Image by David Mark from Pixabay

Thought for the Day

Life is the canvas given to you by the Creator; paint a mural you would like to see, like, admire, and present to the world everyday. Destiny can be your creation when you work incessantly, believing vehemently in yourself and your dreams. So, how about creating a Masterpiece?

Kay S

Foreword

"Midnight Musings" is a collection of poetries and quotes written during my midnight rendezvous with the Universe and my spiritual guide. I have always been of the strong belief that the Universe does pass on messages of great masters for the seeker of truth and knowledge of the beyond. Having said that I also sincerely believe in the lesson I got from the master of my soul, Khan Saab and Guru, my revered Baba Jaan who always made me believe strongly that one has to read their own book to get to the truth about life and its purpose. It is but a few who are capable of doing this and in my endeavor to read my own book to find my purpose, I believe these learnings have been passed on to me through heavenly providence. I am only an instrument, a pen that writes, but my Master, the God within is the ink that flows through me and inspires my thoughts to put them down into words on paper. This is my very humble attempt to put out my thoughts as poetry or quotes hoping to do justice to his reason for creating me. I do believe I have found my purpose to make a difference in this world and I try to do so through various endeavors of mine, writing being one of them. I do sincerely hope that you shall enjoy reading them if you have picked this up as a choice and I do hope they will inspire you to a certain extent at least. In case you have, my heartfelt gratitude to you, my lovely reader. God bless you all with abundance of good health, happiness, prosperity, and success in all that you choose to do and every journey you choose to take in life. Happy Reading!

Kay S

Thought for the Day

There are times in life where you must stand alone to hold ground for a generation to benefit from. If you can and you do, you have the tight mantra for success. It's tough to keep trying; but, it's the hardest to say, 'I failed!' The lone tree shall flower and bear fruits. You are almost there at the finish line; keep trying!

Kay S

Thought for the Day

Words have temperature, use them judiciously. You can present them as a bouquet, a wreath or a garland. A bouquet signifies life, wreath is for death and a garland for prayer or honor. Be conscientious!

Kay S

WORDS

Words are all I have left deep within me,
To express my heartfelt gratitude to thee,
Like a river often and sometimes a creek,
They flow from my brain's private retreat!

Emotions, feelings, and expressions too,
Find their way in communique with you,
Made of simple and complex ones or two,
Sentences made of different words for you!

I endeavor forever to unravel and present,
A multitude of thoughts that are at play,
In a story, a poem, or sometimes a quote,
For words are all I have to freely give away.

Thought for the Day

Live life like a water bubble, attached yet detached. Nothing is permanent in life. Everything is transient in nature, they evolve or devolve. Change is the only constant. Rejoice in the moment. Spread joy and happiness around.

Kay S

MOM

Tender feelings laced with unconditional love,
All that she can hold in her tender heart to show,
Teaching you to always fight your challenges too,
Standing constantly strong behind to empower you.

Burning the night oil numerous times, she waits,
For you as you study on those long exam nights,
Readily there to help whenever you might need,
Never intruding but letting you strive to succeed.

Mothers are indeed kind fairies in disguise,
Sometimes springing an unassuming surprise,
Imparting knowledge with all things so wise,
While protecting you from evil prowling eyes.

I bow down to all of you Guardian Angels today,
For supporting your kids, guiding them all the way,
Never doubting for a minute in the power of Love,
You are blessed by the Supreme from up above.

*PS: Dedicated to my mother, Late Rajalakhsmi
Srinivasan who has been my inspiration.*

Thought for the Day

We are like beautiful sunflowers in the garden of life; we fail to realize this truth. Each dawn comes with a new hope for new dreams and a promise that the night shall pass for the light to shine upon you. Keep blooming. There's hope, hope and more Hope!

Kay S

DAYBREAK

Far away in the horizon you paint your canvas so,
As the dawn yearns for the sun to put on a show,
One world wakes up, one slips into slumber slow,
As witness, the blue sky watches you come and go!

Memories of places such lived many years ago,
With each sunrise a journey begins, either fast or slow,
I begin to absorb your beautiful colors as you rise,
Painting a picture in my heart with great surprise.

Oh beautiful dawn mine, pray do paint my canvas away,
With comrades singing along gleefully, do hold me sway,
When darkness transforms to light slowly paving way,
With bright sunshine, you surely do brighten our day.

Thought for the Day

The sun shines eternally, not to just chase away darkness but enrich mankind, flora, and fauna. Aspire to be like the sun by brightening the world around you and enriching the lives you touch. Life is too precious to pass off as a Nobody. Rise and Shine; Be counted!

Kay S

BURJ KHALIFA

I dare to rise above the looming dense clouds,
I beckon you to come and try do so too,
Life is hard, we all know that is so true,
I remain strong to show, you can be too.

Clouds of doubt will always surround you,
To hinder your path in what you try to do,
Believe in facts you already know are true,
The Universe shall then leave for you a clue.

People at random might try to defeat you,
Misguide you just to see that you are blue,
This too shall pass and you will sail through,
Shining like the stars all the year through!

**Dedicated to my home away from home, Dubai.*

Thought for the Day

The beauty of each sunrise is that it comes back each day. The mystery and beauty of life is to appreciate it because you were lucky to see it again. Each dawn brings renewed hope, opportunities, beginnings, and a chance to make it a better day or be a better version of yourself. Endeavour to bounce back and be the change that you would like to see.

Kay S

DAWN OF HOPE

The day dawns on us with the sun's rays filtering,
Through flimsy folds of curtains meandering,
Waking me to a sight beautiful and charming,
Birds of variety with all their might chirping.

I rise with renewed hope and energy to start,
With feelings of a beautiful day in my heart,
As a smile crosses my face seeming reminiscent,
Of memories lasting, but bygone and present.

Dark nights do pass, the day gently dawns,
Troubles shall ebb to erase all your frowns,
Happiness shall indeed knock on your door,
Boosting spirits up fulfilling desires galore.

With a spring in my step and demeanor joyous,
I step onto the lawns of the blooming azaleas,
The dewdrops on leaves bring upon thoughts anew,
A new dawn, a new day, a new life waits for you.

Thought for the Day

Your life cannot be an option for anyone. It is a precious gift to you from the creator. Realize this truth and cherish it. Rejoice in the beauty of each and every moment because life and time are transient like dewdrops on petals. They evolve whether you do or not. Resolve to re-discover and re-invent to be a better version of yourself each day.

Kay S

EVOLVE

Life is but an evolution of all experiences,
Some your own some from others choices,
Nevertheless, they are lessons to be learnt,
For it is better to be careful than be burnt.

Every day is a memory etched in Time,
Not to wither as a flower but to remain,
In the annals of all books in this Universe,
Recording thoughts and feelings as memoirs.

Fear not for death, the end is but a given,
Your soul dies only to find another haven,
Where you'll be born to exist and create again,
Scripting a new tale that'll never be in vain!

Thought for the Day

The Universe works with you to make your dreams come true, but only if you are true to them. Achievement of your goal requires single-minded devotion and razor-sharp focus. Procrastination and Complacency will get you nowhere. The day is today and the time is now. Rise and Shine!

Kay S

TIME, A TEACHER

Life is like an Oyster, and you are the pearl,
You collect more dust, as much as you swirl.
As obscure as you are, so unique you will be,
Pay no heed to naysayers, let barking dogs be.

All you see at times maybe trials and tribulations,
What I see in front of me is an object of adulation.
I've seen everyone's past and I am in the present,
For I am who you call Time, I need no consent.

Do look within yourself for you shall then find,
A lovely serene abode that shall calm your mind.
Believe there's good too, evil is not always at play,
For I'm omniscient as Time, seeming hard I fade away!

Thought for the Day

Numerous dreams may have perished, many plans shelved, many hearts broken, or many souls separated engulfing you like the darkness of the night. But, there's always sunrise heralding dawn just as it will be in your lives. You have been given a template to script your story; it's up to you to make it a success or not. The weak perish; the tough get going to conquer the next mountain. The darkness shall pass.

Kay S

DREAMS AND ASPIRATIONS

Dreams I conjure up to conquer the world,
Make it to stage awaiting for curtains to unfurl,
Credits score slowly move up on the screen,
Gently revealing the actor's name as mine!

Aspirations I built over a period of time,
Building blocks in this journey of mine,
Hoping to reach that destination screen,
Success they call it, for me bliss so serene.

Revolt I do for all that's wrong in the world,
Believing that I can be the change to unfold,
Portraying characters from lesser known folklore,
I choose to narrate stories that people ignore.

Dreams and aspirations take the driver's seat,
To guide our vehicle of choice for this life's feat,
I shall aspire to persevere to win in this strife,
And stop not for nothing is impossible in life.

Dedicated to an upcoming actor, my Godson, Maahir Mohiuddin.

Thought for the day

When your intentions are pure, your faith is unshakeable and affirmations positive, the Universe presents ways to fulfill your dreams. When you reach that stage of ecstasy, stay firmly rooted to the ground never forgetting how you got there. It takes moments for the Supreme to take away what took years to achieve if ego and pride overrules humility. Stay humble!

Kay S

REDEMPTION

Shower your blessings on me, wash my dirt away,
Let me remain a lily that holds your mind at sway,
Water reminiscent of life's truth of a transient way,
To face challenges head on being stoic and brave.

Malign me away, paint me as dark as you want,
All you say and do shall be adjudged as just a rant,
Your greed for wealth and fame can be a penchant,
This is not a path for me that shall ever enchant.

Pristine pure I remain akin to the lily that I am,
Spreading happiness and joy no matter how I am,
Wallow yourself as you may in fame and the glam,
I'll remain resilient on the lovely path I am on.

Thought for the Day

The dark clouds of uncertainty may be unsettling, but the river of hope is always eternal. Always keep your hopes alive. Hope helps to remain confident of a better tomorrow. Be optimistic, be hopeful

Kay S

SILVER LINING

Dark clouds with silver lining hiding the bright sun,
Is it time for day to pass or is this just for some fun?
The horizon looks tired and weary at the end of day,
Painting a scene, you seem to be carrying along your way.

Dark clouds your silver lining always proves me wrong,
Every time I feel sullen, you inspire me to sing a song,
Off goes the lows to rise up highs in my heart and mind,
Banishing all my inner fears, worry or musings of any kind.

When I see your silver lining, I learn to live from you,
For you rise every day seeming bright, fresh and new,
I watch the beautiful colors you paint from up above,
Each time I realize, a world full of beauty and love.

© Anna Ivanova from NounProject.com

Thought for the Day

Your character is defined by your conduct.
Decorum, dignity, discipline are not options
or choices for multiple choice questions.
First impressions matter; leave a lasting
impression that is pleasant not repulsive

Kay S

CAGED

Strings of fairy lights I am, enclosed in a cage,
Trying to chase this darkness as if I'm in a daze,
Suffocated I feel in such a confining contraption,
Wish you humans understood this very emotion!

Bunched up fairy lights I am, imprisoned in jail,
Invented by human beings to control me, but fail,
I am indeed puny and maybe a puppet to you all,
But I am the light you need to avoid a nasty fall.

Strings of fairy lights I am, just trapped in a cage,
I yearn to be free again and live life on the edge,
I have but a short time until all my fuses blow up,
Won't you just let me shine before my time is up?

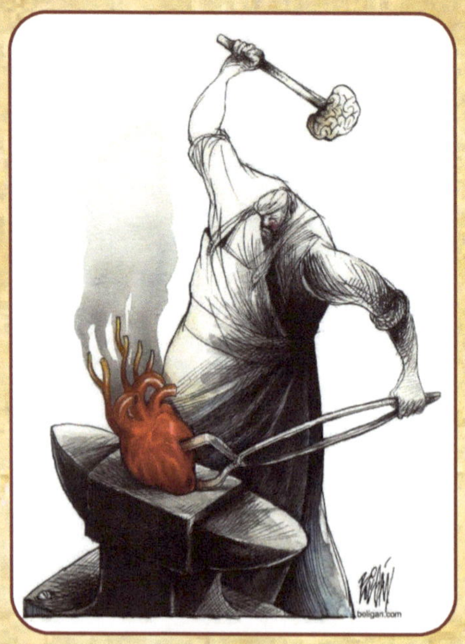

Thought for the Day

Common belief is that a person dies when breathing ceases. Fact is people cease to exist mentally the instant they become selfish, self-centered and reject the power of the Universe. Negativity attracts darkness while positivity brings upon light. May you always be engulfed by the brightness of positivity to emit further, across the world you live in.

Kay S

THE BUTCHER'S BLOCK

My heart lay alive upon a butcher block,
Waiting to be crushed into a meatball,
I see his brain seems off control today,
Hammering all my heart's desires away.

The butcher's block lay cruelly asunder,
Watching me struggle to just live a while,
My heart bleeds for all those bygone days,
As he mercilessly begins to chop me away.

The human mind has turned into child's play,
As though it were but a toy to circumstances,
In his hands I see created a horror of sordid emotions,
Devoid of empathy, I see an evil man enter the fray.

Take control of your mind as you diligently can,
Turn it into a Haven of love and not such scorn,
You'll then see the beautiful garden within my heart,
Flowers blooming from the beauty of my thoughts.

Do not destroy my heart, turn your hate away,
I'd like to live to enjoy all my children at play,
Do change your mind, I beseech, move away from the evil flock,
Let me live to thrive happily, away from this butcher's block.

***Dedicated to my eminent Cardiologist, Dr. Vivek Jawali,
who keeps my heart healthy; his resident intern who
created this and his entire team.*

Krish Mahalingam

Thought for the Day

The process of ageing begins in the mind and the body follows. Keep the innocenceand vitality of the kid in you alive to live life with vigor. Keep the curiosity alive to discover the mysteries of the world. Remain a child at heart forever and seek knowledge to enrich yourself. Learning is unto death and in death is a new learning.

Kay S

UNWIND

I flow along, staying calm, goading you to sing a song,
Come with me or ride over me on a journey not too long,
A sight of beauty shall then unravel for you to capture too,
A memory, a precious moment that I promise to gift to you.

Along my journey, I cross paths with the downtrodden too,
Taking them along, I drift away for them to enjoy the view,
Look into their eyes, you will find a world with a vision anew,
Full of wonder and hope with dreams of a brighter day too.

Flow with me, saunter along, I assure you serenity and grace,
To adapt and practice in your life, which has now become a race,
You rush along each day abysmally ignoring the beauty around,
I entice you to lose yourself in the gorgeous and pristine environs.

I flow along, staying calm, gently goading you to sing a song,
Bask with me in the sun's warmth or just enjoy nature's song,
Let yourself go, experience my serenity, there's nothing wrong,
You need to unwind to face life each day to just remain strong.

Thought for the Day

There will be times when your body cannot listen to what your mind and soul wants. It is important and imperative to know your strengths, weaknesses, limitations and abilities. Each one of us has our limitations and threshold of tolerance. We need to sometimes slow down to rejuvenate, recuperate, repair and restore our heart, mind, body, and soul. You need to heal yourself before healing others. A sound mind exists in a sound body. Love yourself, care for yourself, heal yourself. You are precious.

Kay S

PEEK-A-BOO

Peek-a-Boo you do play with me, lovely lady of the sky,
Blue blanket to envelop you who help you on your sly,
Crimson colors appear far on the cheeks of the horizon,
Seems like you had something to do with the setting sun!

Pine trees pine away trying to rise to feel your milky skin,
Shirking away from their touch, you look down and grin,
As bodyguards, the dark clouds protect you all night long,
You grow beautiful each day becoming the muse of a song!

Peek-a-Boo, my fair lady, give me a chance I beseech you,
Let me serenade, describe you, and then dance with you,
You are but a visitor for me for just a fortnight a month,
Seducing me you disappear with me stuck in a labyrinth!

Thought for the Day

Life is an ocean of unlimited possibilities and unknown adversities. Overconfidence and disbelief will sink you; confidence and faith will help you stay afloat. You can choose to be the Titanic or the Noah's Ark. Your choices definite you.

Kay S

THE BRIDGE OF LIFE

Sauntering along ridges and slopes, I flow along today,
Along the bridge of life alone, I've come a very long way,
As I look back at years passed, my thoughts seem astray,
Inner battles of my mind and heart seem busy at play.

Years of rife and strife I had, treated with a pinch of salt,
Staying grounded all the time, conscious not to ever exalt,
I finally come to a decision to part, and people are appalled,
Making me wonder if living my life is somehow my fault?!

Eons passed since I felt alive as now I blissfully seem to be,
Frolicking and sailing along your banks, I am just being me,
I continue along making my choices, I no more am naive,
For I have chosen to live again crossing that bridge of life!

Thought for the Day

Two negatives turn positive only in math, never in life. Never reduce yourself to be someone you despise. Life is about being happy, proud and content with who you are when you see your reflection in the mirror, the rest is a mirage. Stay positive.

Kay S

GLEEFUL LIGHTS

Gleeful Lights, you cheer me up on a dreary cold night,
Painting me pretty with your color and your bright light,
My walls of stone are bland indeed, not a very pretty sight,
Seeing myself adorned this way, my thoughts take flight.

Gleeful Lights, you make me feel warm and cheerful today,
I urge you to be with me forever to brighten me each day,
I hope my handsome owner too feels the very same way,
And help my dreams come true by letting you just stay.

Gleeful Lights, charming and bright you have carved a niche,
To be around people of the world no matter poor or rich,
I hope my plans to always shine will clear without a hitch,
For I shall never be bland again nor will you have a glitch.

Thought for the Day

Nature and the Universe is the creator's gift to mankind unraveling itself in unimaginable ways. The colors on your palette already exist in the Universe. We can admire, appreciate and accept all truths when we widen our horizon of thoughts beyond ourselves. Empty your brain like a cup each day. Learning is a journey, not a destination. Stay hungry for the knowledge of the Universe.

Kay S

FROM AN ABYSS

The emptiness of these walls seemed to beckon,
As my visions in mind's deep crevices awaken,
Of streams, waterfalls, and mountains unshaken,
Began then a creation on a wall plain, forsaken.

Like the creator weaves magic with his wand,
Began the strokes of a brush with adept hand,
Beauty with serenity emerged on barren land,
As time slipped through our day just like sand.

Passion became a river, Love became a waterfall,
My strength was a mountain that shall never fall,
As my dreams took off, like a boisterous sky fall,
Complete you are hills, lakes, and scenic waterfall.

From an abyss, I shall always arise, into it I'll perish,
I exist in the emptiness of it and gloriously flourish,
I am not a dish that every normal human can relish,
I am definitely not a comrade to the evil and selfish.

***Inspired by a mural by Rushabh Nagraj and Megha Shankar*

Thought for the Day

Life is your canvas, paint the mural you would want to see and admire each day. In the end, it is the choices you make that define you. Make the choice to discard toxic people in your lives and surround yourself with positive energy. Destiny is your creation, let us create a masterpiece.

Kay S

A BRUSH WITH LIFE

Painting my thoughts, I seem to have a brush with my life,
Brushes of mine as I liberally use during my rife and strife,
Giving vibrant colors to my mind, you do tirelessly strive,
Giving images to all emotions, you seem to decipher life.

Myriad emotions, dreams, and thoughts gently find a way,
As you pick colors from the palette to busy yourself away,
The canvas gently transforms into a vivid movie scene,
You depict the vagaries of life, all chaotic and also serene.

A brush with life I do have each time I dare to take a risk,
That's a feeling you portray with each stroke ever so brisk,
At times when you carve a story, I seem to be your muse,
Most times I do run to you to de-stress, unwind, or defuse.

Thought for the Day

Each day reveals itself to you like a miracle for you are awake with a new opportunity to make a difference in the world around you. There's someone out there who never woke up from eternal sleep. Humility, faith and gratitude are virtues that shall always protect you. Rejoice and celebrate life. Have faith in yourself and the power of the supreme.

Kay S

THROUGH THE BLINDS

Through the window blinds, a new dawn emerges,
Seeming to reveal our life's enthralling pages,
The sun paints away myriad hues of colors in stages,
That looks like parakeets escaping from their cages.

Your presence heralds the dawn of a bright new life,
Feels as though a cocoon transforms into a butterfly,
I then become a part of nature's melodious symphony,
Accepting your subtle presence, I forget all my agony.

Through the venetian blinds, a new morn beckons me,
As the morn breeze gently caresses branches of a tree,
The tender flower shies away hearing the buzz of a bee,
As I yearn to feel your strong arms gently hugging me.

© Image by günter from Pixabay

Thought for the Day

Each one of us is a unique masterpiece of the creator with unique thoughts, actions, abilities and masterplan for our lives and the Universe. Our duty is to realize, recognize, reconcile, find and execute that masterplan. When we endeavor to achieve something and emit positive affirmations, the Universe shall conspire to make it a reality. Search within, find your masterplan and design your legacy!

Kay S

UNIQUE

I am a precious pearl who my parents gave birth to,
My dreams are indeed to be a priceless pearl to you,
Unique in my ways I am and sometimes hard too,
For the right person indeed, melt like the wax I do.

Each person is so special that comes into my life,
Fills me with awe, slicing my disbelief like a knife,
I wonder at times endlessly about life and its strife,
Could I cross this raging life's sea being so naive?

Unique in our ways we are indeed, like pastels on a tray,
Yet we row the boat of life, only to simply sail away,
Creating memories to brood upon on our dreary days,
Bravely we carry on with life to go our separate ways!

Thought for the Day

Love is a complete yet infinite and incomplete circle of life, never demanding, forever unconditional, undemanding, and unfinished. True love is being selfless to remain in the shadow to brighten the world of the one you love and rejoice in their happiness. You attain the bliss of the Supreme in the soul of your beloved, a rare occurrence in the world. The hearts of such souls beat in unison and see no boundaries as a world remains oblivious.

Kay S

ROAD LESS TRAVELED

I take the forbidden road of love that leads me to you,
The morning sun beckons me with its seductive hue,
Dark clouds of doubt try to dampen my lilting mood,
The sun plays mischievous truant as I begin to brood.

The journey on this road less traveled is tough I reckon,
Your memories and love for me seems to gently beckon,
I start off with a zeal picking up pace fearing to slacken,
Yearning to be safe in your arms, lest the world does awaken.

Tender hues of color on sky, pray inform my beloved too,
Clear the haze and lead me to him under this sky so blue,
Guide me on this path deftly for my life depends on you,
Cottony clouds, do wait to pour until my dreams come true.

Thought for the Day

One minute of anger weakens the immune system by 4 to 5 hours and one minute of laughter boosts immune system for 24 hours. Patience and composure during anger will help avoid days of sorrow and hurt. Words have temperature; they can serenade, salvage, scald or scar. Mindfulness, patience, compassion, and Empathy are virtues to be practiced for a better brighter life and to cherish relationships. Be mindful before you speak for a bullet fired can only kill not return to the barrel.

Kay S

SCARS REMAIN

You leave me behind ruthlessly to deal with my loss,
Causing gentle havoc within me each time you cross,
I saunter along melancholically pretending to be fine,
The bitter truth of life is that my ugly scars remain.

I reminisce upon the happiness you do always bring,
Each morning diligently when you do come visiting,
Seems as if my thoughts each day are just a scattering,
And our union each time seems like many gypsies wandering.

I let my scars remain on, for they remind me of you,
Like your love for me is unconditional, ever so true,
Each day when you return into my outstretched arms,
You do scar me again with no remorse or qualms.

Thought for the Day

Each one of us have arrived into this world with a script of our own to serve a purpose to mankind. The Herculean task is to recognize and fulfill that purpose. Elevate yourself, your thoughts, your actions to enact your script to serve mankind and humanity. Leave a legacy for generations to follow. Living for yourself is easy, living for others is pure bliss.

Kay S

PANGS OF DESIRE

My emotions have calmed down as these waves today,
As you bade goodbye to me to travel to a land far away,
I shall wait for the dawn to arise to wipe my tears away,
Hold me close one last time as I hold my feelings at bay.

Pangs of desire rock my soul as the waves hit on rocks,
At times chirping away like those birds flying in flocks,
My feelings seem to hum like a buzzing swarm of bees,
I collapse on my bed like a corpse trying to fall asleep.

Bidding good-bye, I wait for you by the lonely banks,
Filling my mind with hope like water gallons in tanks,
My heavy heart suddenly does release a very loud howl,
As the ocean's silence seems to soothe my hurting soul.

Thought for the Day

Life is a journey that you can enrich or just travel listlessly. You are born alone, you leave alone. In between, you have co-passengers who leave at their destination. Gain wisdom, practice humility, immerse yourself in the Supreme. Don't feel lonely, accept and love your solitariness. You need to live with your company for life.

Kay S

THE LAKE

I flow as tears through your eyes, kind soul, hear me out,
Before the world ignores me to succeed in drying me out,
You don't know me for I'm neither famous nor with the clout,
I am a tiny lake in the hills, waiting for you to hear me out.

I see you waiting alone by my banks, just brooding away,
I feel the emotions deep within you trying to find a way,
I reach out to touch to console, calm your inner being too,
You withdraw from me, not knowing I could help you too.

As your tears flow unhindered, I collect unbeknownst to you,
I'm the lake that stem from feelings flowing from within you,
Your inner self knows me well, wish you'd recognize too,
I urge you kindly to keep flowing just as you need me to.

Thought for the Day

Life is carved through trials and tribulations, not a smooth highway. It depends on how much you absorbed, accepted, assimilated, and articulated its learnings in everyday life to carve you into a fine human being. May life give you the opportunity to be an amazing sculptor of a beautiful sculpture – "YOU."

Kay S

SUNFLOWER

I bloom for you, O morning sun, please do look at me,
I frolic in joy and smile away as I attract a queen bee,
She sniffs away for nectar, hoarding it to make honey,
Through this labor humans do make a lot of money.

Kids have come on a field trip to see my friends today,
As they come to admire me, I am a Sunflower I say,
Seeds of mine are useful too, I can save your hearts,
I sacrifice petals for oil to use on your painful parts.

I'm a sunflower golden yellow, and I feel so attractive,
Blooming at early sunrise, I strive to be fresh and active,
The gardener comes to water me with a kind motive,
He loves to show me off, hence, I strive forever to live.

Watch me bloom and smile away, for it's a new dawn today,
Fill your hearts with hope and drive all your worries away,
I may just be a flower blooming with the morning sun,
I strive to remind, you are special to a precious someone.

Thought for the Day

Sometimes in life, there comes a time when you feel everything is pulling you down to bury you deep under. This, is the time when you should muster up courage and gusto to surge ahead like a typhoon to capture the attention of the Universe, to prove yourself as a power to reckon with. You were created and destined for success, not failure. Realize this ultimate truth, for God helps those who help themselves. Rise and shine...A world awaits your radiance.

Kay S

RAYS OF HOPE

Filtering through the shady curtain of leaves,
The sunshine falls upon the wilting lilies,
Pitying their plight as I walk down the slopes,
I hope to find solace in the sun's rays of hope.

Your gentle rays graze my tender pale skin,
Making me feel as if I am a dainty Queen,
I bask in your presence as if you're my King,
I steal a sly glance when you're not looking.

Gentle rays of sunshine, pray fill me with hope,
Each time I falter, I wish you'd help me to cope,
With each decision I make, always be my rope,
Hold me tight just in case I slip down the slope.

Thought for the Day

Do your own soul searching; reflect upon yourself before reflecting upon others. You will find your secrets and your manuscript within. Act on improving your role within the Universe. Act on improving your role in this Universe and mankind shall follow. Positivity breeds positive energy, negativity exudes negative energy. Stay positive, stay kind.

Kay S

REFLECTIONS

I'm the picture you paint from choices you've made,
Reflections of your mind creating a soft subtle shade,
On clear days like this sky, when there'll be no clouds,
On a gloomy day, I appear conforming to your moods.

Choices define us and hence are constant companions,
Painfully goading us rightly to avoid painful reunions,
Stall if you must, to choose the right things
For it's you who will need to suffer if troubles are rife.

Reflections I mirror from feelings and thoughts within,
I'm the ice on winter nights, who floats on lakes, so thin,
I break easily with a soft push or just with a gush of wind,
If you keep your thoughts clear, I can reflect your mind.

Thought for the Day

Every moment of your life is metered, spend it wisely. Every thought of yours is reciprocal. So, manifest goodness, happiness and prosperity. The Masters of the Universe are life's teachers, respect them. Wisdom and humility are virtues, not luxuries. Imbibe them in daily life and abundance shall be yours. Open your heart, mind, body and soul to the goodness in this Universe.

Kay S

SHORES OF LIFE

My journey ends today as the yonder shores beckon me,
I need to bid good-bye to travels, leave memories behind,
I look forward to my newfound freedom and the bonhomie,
Ready to adapt a new rhythm, away from the lame grind.

The sun shines brightly, before bidding adieu to the day,
Off to travel to farther lands to drive their darkness away,
Bringing hopes of new beginnings or maybe old endings,
A chance for a rendezvous at dusk or some surprise meetings.

As I reach the shores of life where my heart solely belongs,
I yearn to script a new beginning, just to right my wrongs,
I gallantly march further and disembark from my past life,
Promising to the Universe to never ever give up in my strife.

Thought for the Day

A small word of love will mean the world to a hurting soul like a piece of log for a drowning person. Kindness, empathy, understanding and compassion costs nothing. You never know when you will need any of them. Be mindful of your words and actions. Mindfulness is a priceless virtue to practice.

Kay S

LITTLE PLEASURES

A tender smile, a warm embrace, and a look is all I need,
I do feel happy, enchanted, and on top of the world indeed,
A subtle fear of the unknown does lurk each time we meet,
I feel like the mat is being pulled from beneath my feet.

I yearned for moments to be alone away from the world,
With memories to warm my heart, on dreary days so cold,
You invaded my mind and senses, captured my dear heart,
Unbeknownst to me, you capture my soul to never depart.

Little pleasures have always been my life's greatest win,
Making me dizzy with happiness like a top on a spin,
Relationships can be fragile like a spider's web so fine,
Let's promise to nurture them with thoughts we do define.

Words conveyed in silence always speak volumes to me,
Decoding them I gaze into your eyes knowing you agree,
With no questions or promises, we shall forever remain,
In each other's heart no matter what, come hail or sunshine.

© Dr. Vivek Jawali

Thought for the Day

The clouds will pass, the moon of life shall appear bright and you will shine like the star you are destined to be. You just need to believe in yourself, have faith in the powers of the Universe, stay resilient and focused and persevere. Good things do come to people who wait.

Kay S

REMNANTS OF NIGHT

The calm night bids goodbye leaving droplets upon me,
Seeming like strands of shiny pearls, gently enticing me,
I travel back in time to when none existed but just him,
When I gazed into his eyes thinking it was just a dream.

Dewdrops are remnants of the night, which I spent with you,
Tender whispers of endearment that left a colorful hue,
Transporting me to yonder lands, with undeniable allure
When I succumbed to my feelings, so strong and pure.

I shall wait for the night to feel your warm embrace again,
Your presence brings me pleasure and erases away my pain,
I step into a magical paradise each time you become mine,
I calm down to note my heart humming a tune ever so fine.

Thought for the Day

Every moment of your life is metered, spend it wisely. Every thought of yours is reciprocal. So, manifest goodness, happiness and prosperity. The masters of the Universe are life's teachers, respect them. Wisdom and humility are virtues, not luxuries. Imbibe them in daily life and abundance shall be yours. Open your heart, mind, body and soul to the goodness in this Universe.

Kay S

REMINISCENCE

Embers of your presence does gently remain with me behind,
The abyss in me lingers as I think about you in rewind,
Reminiscence, an essence of my calm and serene mind,
As I learn to live and throw caution to the errant wind.

The birch trees stare away a witness to our rendezvous,
The pine trees pine away to experience your bliss too,
Oblivious to our presence, the fir trees remain green,
The cottony clouds stoically watch as observers refrain.

The burning desire of your presence slowly dies down,
Myriad stars begin to shine in company of the moon,
I withdraw stealthily to erase your remnants on my skin,
Trying hard to hide my trauma from my own kith and kin.

Thought for the Day

Destiny demands decisiveness. When you know your goal and the path to reach it, procrastination cannot be your companion. Clarity of thoughts and actions will lead you to success. Rise to every situation confidently and script our destiny. May the forces be with you.

Kay S

BREAKING BARRIERS

Revealing whims and fancies galore,
Weaving them into a cute folklore,
Of people who often shut their door,
For they've no guts to handle anymore.

Frolic away with a spring in your step,
You'll have journeyed on life's fine trip,
As you go ahead reach greater heights,
Ignore them as though we do ugly mites.

Your thoughts maybe sometimes truant,
But should never be a blaming lament,
String words in a necklace, so eloquent,
To impress none, but just be frank and blunt.

Cathartic acts have been proven to free your soul,
From memories that seem to remain on the prowl,
As they dig away subtly at your inner peace,
I urge you to ignore and do as your heart would please.

Thought for the Day

Treat your brain like a cup. Empty your cup each day if you want to fill it with knowledge and wisdom of the Universe. A filled cup overflows, the empty one fills. Let the thirst and desire for knowledge and life remain eternal. Always strive to shine like the lighthouse leading people into light through darkness.

Kay S

WHIMSICAL THOUGHTS

My cuppa fills to the brim with all the joy you bring,
Goading me to break my eerie silence to merrily sing,
I bask in subtle notes of music that enter my realm,
As you begin to sing a song from my favorite film.

I reminisce upon days, does not seem so long ago,
As a dainty damsel when I had held his imagination so,
Frolicking in the sun, I did conjure up mischiefs galore,
Listening to mom's witty tales and grandma's folklore.

My whimsical mind is filled with sweet memories I cherish,
I feel cheerful yet maudlin, but I'm filled with flourish,
On dreary days that are a few, I dare to dream and wish,
And off I go into the ocean of life swimming like a fish.

© Image by annca from Pixabay

Thought for the Day

Each time you hurt a kind soul, the Universe is maintaining checks and balances. Every sinner will rise higher only to come crashing down. Bide your time, smile and be patient. If you are lucky, you will see the downfall of the ones who hurt you. Goodness shall prevail. The justice of the Supreme is unbiased, untainted and pure; it sees or knows no relationship.

Kay S

SANDS OF TIME

Stolen by the Universe, time gently passes away,
While you're being busy keeping troubles at bay,
Each second indeed is your blessing from above,
Chosen for you, they're like gems from a treasure trove.

Time is a precious gift and I am giving you my time,
Something that can be stolen and still not be a crime,
Moments turn into memories to stay with us behind,
Turning into memoirs to narrate with thoughts in rewind.

Moments I spend with you, I hope are special to you,
I decorate them with love as I present them to you,
On drab dreary days, I hope they cheer and keep you,
In the best of your spirits to help you sail through.

© **Image by Susanne Jutzeler, Schweiz, from Pixabay**

Thought for the Day

Walk with pride, live with dignity, respect and love yourself. Self-love and self-esteem ensures the person across you is obligated to treat you with respect. When you neglect yourself, the world will neglect you for you become redundant to yourself and the world. Rise and shine, be counted.

Kay S

SCENT OF YOU

Your heady scent slowly invades my tired senses,
As sinister clouds loom bringing about darkness,
I withdraw gently within to try to protect my soul,
As the wind blows ruthlessly emitting a loud howl.

Your thoughts begin to disrupt my ever serene mind,
Bringing up fond memories like a film in rewind,
I retire into my balcony to see a sunset to unwind,
Your heady scent pervades my senses again I find.

Let me be in a solitary state, let me be for some time,
As I gently gather all my thoughts, ever so sublime,
I shall be back in your arms, when it is your time,
I do hope you respect my wish, and not feel it's a crime.

Thought for the Day

The long struggles, the endless sleepless nights, the unending challenges all come to fruition when your faith is strong and intentions are pure. Do your bit with diligence and sincerity, the results will be delivered by the Universe. The best is yet to come, this is only the beginning. Keep striving.

Kay S

YEARNINGS

As I look over the railings of my barren balcony,
The sun slowly sets, leaving me in harmony,
With a very subtle reminder of the day you leave,
As my eyes fail to hide the melancholic dark hue.

I saunter back to see you still in my bed,
I sit by you gently touching your forehead,
You open your eyes slowly,, pulling me close softly,
Melting me in your arms as you hold me gently.

I know I'll miss you more when you are gone,
Waking up to an empty home each and every morn,
But I shall endeavor to not still feel so forlorn,
As I look forward to you on a new dawn.

Yearnings of ours, so subtle yet so strong,
Do hold me frozen, many a times for long,
I wish to feel the same as we move along,
Hoping to script our life's melodious song.

Thought for the Day

People come into your life for a reason, as lessons or experiences and some in the form of Angels to enrich or augment your lives. Appreciate, behold and cherish them. These are the ones that may not smile with you, but they will surely cry for you and with you. These are your soulmates. May you always be blessed with one.

Kay S

SOULMATE

You send me cryptic messages, you tend to entice me so,
I dream of meeting you some day, you do behold me so,
I share my thoughts, my dreams, and shortcomings with you,
You are my soothsayer at time and also my Soulmate too!

Happiness and pain have been but my dearest companions,
Each time I felt ecstatic, life brought myriad commotions,
I kept landing in despair, tried to grapple with emotions,
You stayed to strengthen me though your conversation.

I look forward to your messages your guardian angels,
Brightening my day like the light of a thousand candles,
I await the day when I'm with you, not in such shambles,
The Universe sends your cryptic note as if preamble.

***Dedicated to the Master of my Soul*

Thought for the Day

"I cannot do it!" You can spend all your precious living moments thinking this OR get up and do something about it. Procrastination is a perfect word for a dictionary for you need to do exactly that to collect and conjure words to build a dictionary. Rise and Shine, Lovelies! A Universe waits for a Star – You!!

Kay S

KALEIDOSCOPE

Pieces of glass bangles, all scattered on the floor,
Beckoning me deftly to bend down on all my fours.
Pick them all I gently did, placed them in a clear cup,
What I saw through glass made me rush to a craft shop.

Into a cylindrical box I then let all the broken pieces fall,
Plugged both sides, then rolled it with pinhole on one end,
Into the hole I peeped to see designs unfold to behold,
A jolt of thought emerged with realization of a special kind.

When life deals a bad set of cards, it seems like the shards,
You may also feel scattered like the pieces of broken glass,
It's up to you to make your mind and believe this shall pass,
Like a kaleidoscope you shall transform to then be a boss.

Thought for the Day

Disperse your presence like fragrance; dissolve your woes like sugar; evolve yourself like a butterfly. Energize your surroundings like the sun, the flowers, the rains. Immerse yourself in the beauty of this earth.

Kay S

LALBAGH

The sky smiles away as the sun rises in the east,
With Bougainvillea and Tabebuias joining the feast,
The waterfall deftly dances a jig feeling so upbeat,
The birds chirp away gleefully completing this feat.

As a gypsy sets out today traversing through my town,
Alone I am he says, I'm not lonely nor do I feel down,
The City of Gardens wakes up to a beauty of its own,
My morning begins to his tales to erase if any frown.

My doctor at heart visits this garden each day at morn,
Capturing sunsets, flora and fauna, or at times a song,
Through their lens I learn to see our city is not a drag,
Merrily, we celebrate the glory of my city's 'LALBAGH.'

PC: Inspired by Dr. Vivek Jawali, a renowned cardiac surgeon and Prof. Ramesh Dutt's photography of Bangalore's Pride, Lalbagh (A Red Garden).

Thought for the Day

The Universe protects those who protect it.
Nature is God's poetry in motion. Accept,
appreciate, assess and augment it with your
presence, respect and care. When you destroy,
you reap destruction. Stay conscientious.

Kay S

POETRY IN MOTION

As you bid goodbye to me to light another world,
I calm down rippling gently, my emotions on hold,
I will rise and flow again to reach my destination,
Where my beloved awaits to meet with time frozen.

The human across barricades is in awe watching me,
Finding serenity in silence giving me some company,
He captures the beauty of our separation on his pricey phone,
As he seems to enamored by your departure alone.

The expanse of my waters does make me a sight to see,
For the world to come over to shores to just watch me,
I blissfully flow along, just happy with this sweet notion,
I inspire people to see me be a poetry in motion.

© Image by Nino Carè from Pixabay

Thought for the Day

You are the author and protagonist of your book called "Life" because it has already been written for you to rewrite. Discover yourself, read your book and rewrite your script. Ask for what you desire, not what you do not wish for. Let each one pen their script. Be the pen that the Supreme uses to write your destiny.

Kay S

BOOKS

New or old, fresh or brittle, maybe big or small,
Manage to capture imaginations, rising ever so tall,
Narrating a story of a sorry bloke who once did fall,
Or just reciting a poem of yore to gently enthrall.

Books of mine that I traveled with to lands afar.
that always left doors of my mind widely ajar,
Giving pleasant experiences and at time bizarre,
Overwhelming sometimes, just like a shooting star.

These amazing books did unravel my soul,
Reminding life's sojourns, so many untold,
Unfolding like bedsheets, each fold by fold,
Presenting odes with panaches to gently behold.

© Image by Narasimha R from Pixabay

Thought for the Day

The heart feels what the eyes see; the mind remembers what the heart feels; the soul remembers what the eyes, heart, and mind do not see, feel, or remember. Kindness and empathy are great virtues to imbibe.

Kay S

BANGLES

Those colorful bangles that adorn your wrist,
Seem to reach out to me wanting to have a tryst,
Where you and I as 'We' may then finally exist,
To be a part of the Universe, nothing to desist.

Come with me, let us go chase the end of a rainbow,
Frolic in the winds, throw caution out of the window,
Let's soar the skies feeling high and dipping so low,
Savoring love one day at a time like a dance so slow.

Your colorful bangles seem to love taunting me to glory,
As though gearing up to write a fairytale or story,
I let you carry me away into a land with no worry,
Knowing I'm in paradise, surely not in any hurry.

*Dedicated to the beautiful bangles-adorned hands of
my darling, Syeda Tahseen.*

Thought for the Day

Life becomes a beautiful journey when we unravel each day like a mysterious gift. In this limited edition of life, remain Unlimited and Unfinished in spreading kindness, compassion, happiness, and empathy.

Kay S

UNFINISHED

Each time you look at me,
Each time you do judge me,
Each time you dismiss me,
I'd like to remind you gently,

I'm perfect in my imperfections,
I am God's Creation in motion,
I'm enthralled by your ignorance,
I am thankful for my resilience.

I'm now endeavoring to just evolve,
I'm also beginning to learn to resolve,
Aware I am indeed I've many miles to travel,
Traverse them I will and remain Unfinished still.

Thought for the Day

String your troubles, tune your sadness, and strum your joys away. Life shall then bloom like a beautiful flower. Rejoice in the existence of everything and the nothingness because the Universe began from an abyss, from nothingness, the nebula. Spread your music far and wide across so the Universe can waltz for you and with you.

Kay S

SYMPHONY OF MUSIC

Silence persists as music invades my senses as a whole,
Your voice resonates loudly, from deep within the soul,
Shakes me out of my reverie as if it was on a prowl,
Words then impact me as if from Universe's Black hole.

My nerves are on edge, my thoughts refuse to budge,
You effortlessly make me forget every single grudge,
Engulfed by words into an abyss of deeper meaning,
I desperately struggle to stabilize, my shaken footing.

The symphony of music, lilting notes, and the vocals pervade,
Precipitating every crevice of my brain, I try hard to evade,
As your resounding voice reaches its highest crescendo,
I gently surrender to its' effervescent and shining bright glow.

*Dedicated to Khan Saab, the Master of my soul with
an amazing voice!*

Thought for the Day

You are your own enemy. When you allow negative elements and thoughts to enter your realm, they corrode your brain, your aura and your personality akin to a rusting iron. An idle wayward mind destroys itself, an active one thrives in positivity.

Kay S

SHROUD OF ECSTASY

I rise over my physical being with a shroud of ecstasy,
Yearning to meet a figment of my own heart's fantasy,
As you rise and set in the horizon far away from me,
My longing to be one with you begins to haunt me.

My waves rise to become a veil hoping to protect you,
From errant souls or evil eyes that seem to beseech you,
I capture your attention as you wait for a brief instance,
Enraptured, I dance merrily with abundant exuberance.

My invisible shroud unveils as you softly bid goodbye,
To yonder lands you go away, in your quest to brighten lives,
Each day I await your return as I lay out my veiled soul,
My nights yawn restlessly in company of the lonely owl.

© Image by Stefan Keller from Pixabay

Thought for the Day

The unending chaos, the long struggling days of hardships, the dragging moments of despair, and the tough challenges all do most certainly end to unveil the beautiful creation called success or the walk to the glorious finish line. After all, it takes many million hammer strokes of a hammer to carve a beautiful sculpture.

Kay S

UNBRIDLED PAIN

Tears do flow shamelessly unhindered,
Not knowing you have but wandered,
Into the horizon, a land of no return,
Where everything is so sad and doomed.

I beseech you earnestly, hoping to hold you again,
But you never seem to hear me or even feel my pain,
I keep waiting for your response, but alas in vain,
You've left to me to a land far, where you shall remain.

You hear not my cries, nor do you see my flowing tears,
For you exist no more, it has been quite a number of years,
I gaze into space yearning to see you, amidst all my fears,
You seem to have moved on just as do all flowing rivers.

It causes me grief and unbearable pain,
As my tears doth flow unhindered again,
I attempt to get some sleep, but in vain,
From my bedside, I see the pouring rain.

My mind seems to be silent, deeply lost in time,
Actions of mine have become like a pantomime,
Glaringly I note reluctantly, the harsh truth remains,
You've wandered so far away, never to return again.

Thought for the Day

Once in a lifetime, you may be lucky to get the opportunity to pursue a purpose that is larger than you, your dream, your desires or your life itself. This is a but a blessing from the Supreme to lead you to a success you never imagined, for the sake of mankind. The path will be tough, full of hardships and requires resilience, patience and passion. If you've found this, your life's purpose has been served.

Kay S

NATURE'S DIAMOND

I hang on to dear life at the edge of leaves and branches,
I guess it's just as though in life you take your chances,
Will I make it through or not is just like life's nuances,
Time will tell whether or not I shall make any advances.

'Tis indeed hard dto hang on to sanity when life's tough,
For the tough get going, when the times are rough,
You need to be resilient and also strong to call out life's bluff,
For you are born to conquer the world, and not be in a cuff.

I watch the world passing by from branches up above,
Hanging on for dear life lest the wind gives me a shove,
It's a chance I'm taking for I believe that I'll not sway,
I'm the diamond dewdrop at dawn merrily shining away.

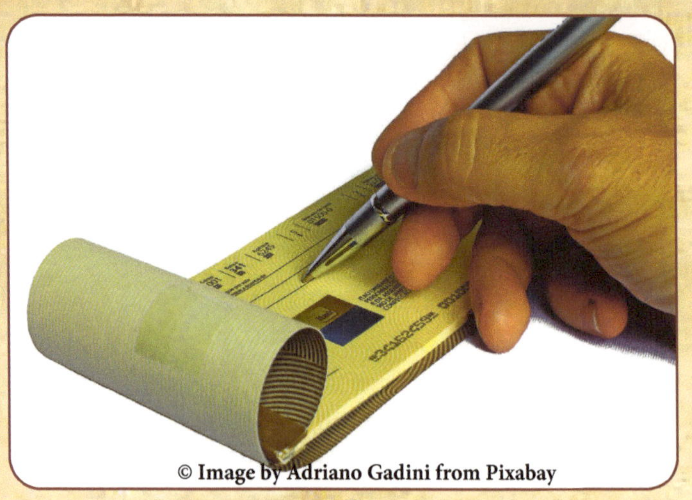

© Image by Adriano Gadini from Pixabay

Thought for the Day

Life is constantly a battle between two choices – right and wrong, do I or don't I, will I or won't I, this way or that way, good or bad. The choice is always yours' one leads to success and makes you happy, the other leads you to doom or misery follows. In the end, you shall lie on the bed you chose and made for yourself. You may not belong to the world, but at least must belong to yourself.

Kay S

THE PAYCHECK

Yearning hands, pending bills and commitments galore,
Rise up to remind me each month knocking on my door,
I respond to them that I acknowledge and I eagerly wait,
For my paycheck to be lying under my boss' paperweight.

He dilly dallies to pay each month as he resorts to blackmails,
"You've not done enough work, I do not see a sale." he wails,
I listen to him with a heavy heart as tears fill my weary eyes,
For diligently working such long hours, why is this my price?

Being an employer is a privilege, I think the universe provides,
To enable the downtrodden and uplift many less fortunate lives,
It's indeed a pity bosses think they can hold employees in check,
As they harass employees each month withholding their cheque.

The paycheck keeps evading me painfully each and every month,
At the cruel hands of viciousness, I try to present a brave front,
My patience wears thin, strength begins to wean slowly away,
As I pray I shall look forward to someday will this cheque away.

© Image by Franck Barske from Pixabay

Thought for the Day

There are no accidents with respect to meeting people; there are merely destined coincidences. The Universe showers its blessings in the form of beautiful souls in your life; there's always a reason or a greater good. The positive energies of these lovely souls around excite and exalt you to dimensions unknown. Embrace, Accept, and Rejoice in this heavenly meeting of souls. Stay blessed always.

Kay S

LAST LULLABY

Come to me my beloved, lie on my lap some time,
Let's recollect memories from days of our prime,
When days belonged to you, and the nights were all mine,
When candlelight dinners did end with goblets of old wine.

I cajole my mind not to drift feeling your tender skin,
I admire your handsome face that had young girls gawking,
As I yearn to feel again those strong arms holding me,
The stormy clouds did herald an unending life so gloomy.

As I hold your lifeless body close to my bosom today,
I feel that you are here with me and not gone far away,
I feel your body, stroke your head, try hard not to cry,
But I know deep within, I must sing your Last Lullaby.

***Dedicated to all Martyrs across the world.*

Thought for the Day

'I' beseech you; 'I' revere You; 'I' surrender to You; 'I' exist in You; 'I' am immersed in You. 'I' am singular while 'You' exist in plurality. 'I' am pride while 'You' are humility personified. By myself, 'I' am just an empty mortal coil; by existing in You and your nothingness, 'I' become part of a whole and encompass the Universe. Humility is a virtue to imbibe and practice. In the end, we need just four shoulders to carry us to our final destination. Be humble, be wise.

Kay S

ME NO MORE

I am me no more, for I now have indeed transformed,
I yearn no more for the mundane, for I am reformed,
Emotions and attachments now, seem a tad too weird,
Guess these are just by-products, when you feel tired.

Tired of hypocrisies, fallacies, and the double standards,
Added to lies that reek from people who have faltered,
I turn myself within to retrospect, not be self-centered,
I endeavor to protect my soul from everything I dread.

Yes! I am me no more for I have transformed and evolved,
I'm a humanist with values rather than a body devolved,
Having chosen to follow a path many would dare not tread,
I proclaim I've enjoyed every moment of the life I have lived.

Praise for the Book

Midnight Musings is not a book you read through and put away. It is something that stays with you leaving an impress that resonates with your own being for a long, long time.

Most of us get so carried away with the mundane business of day-to-day living and surviving all that life throws at us that we seldom find the time to stand and stare as Milton put it. But not Kay, a survivor who has scrambled her way up to a higher plane of being. The world of noise movement and striving fades away as Kay opens hidden windows to new strains of thought and feeling. Kay plumbs her own soul to respond to everyday sights sounds and phenomenon of nature, whether it is daybreak or the night sky. She even has a philosophical response to the Burj Khalifa and its sky piercing height. Every sentence she writes she offers like a gift to the reader. Every line of poetry is rich and resonant with a wealth of meaning and feelings to reach deep into the human soul and trigger a chain of thought about life and living and its underlay of meaning.

Kay is an old soul who has seen the raw edge of life and it has matured and mellowed her thought process and her writing to a depth seldom reached. Her poetry and her daily insights are on one level an admirable masterful flow of language; on another level, they provoke and prod the angst that keeps us human.

As she says in one of her insights - You can present words as a bouquet, a wreath, or a garland. Her easy mastery of the language enables her to express the inexpressible as a bouquet, a wreath or a garland.

Sadiqa Peerbhoy
Advertising Professional, Columnist and Author

About the Book

When the night sets in, the world around me sleeps away slipping into dreams, I slip into an abyss where my thoughts flow from a different dimension forming beautiful verses that manifest into a poem or a quote. This book is a result of my rendezvous with the Universe & my Spiritual master. I withdraw within to introspect, to find myself and peace in the silence of my world. Often, human beings ignore the beauty that exists around, be it in the form of creation, art, or what the eyes sees and the heart, soul & mind combinedly perceive. Poetry, I believe, is an intense, intricate, and inimitable language of each soul, unique yet beautiful. I present this to you for, "Words are all I have to present as a gift to thee!"

Human beings endeavor to attain happiness for tomorrow, forgetting it already exists today, as they are busy chasing their evasive tomorrow. The emptiness of abysmally living without a purpose, amassing materialistic wealth can perish if we imbibe certain virtues such as tolerance, acceptance, compassion and empathy. The attempt of this book is to jostle your mind, cajole your senses, soothe the soul, rake emotions, awaken the kid within while making you smile, laugh, cry, ponder and then become silent to introspect within. This book, written from deep within the soul of a writer who lives life with a higher purpose will take you through myriad moods, emotions, circumstances, feelings, relationships, the everything & nothingness of the universe.

Always remember when there is utter silence, the voice of your soul shall be audible because silence speaks through art, music, creation, the soul, mind, eyes, tears, laughter, happiness, sadness, and then yes, through WORDS!

May your musings speak the language of your soul through, "Midnight Musings." Happy Reading!

www.ingramcontent.com/pod-product-compliance
Lightning Source LLC
Chambersburg PA
CBHW042119150726

48005CB00026B/27